HAPPINESS

JACK UNDERWOOD

Happiness

FABER & FABER

First published in 2015
by Faber & Faber Ltd
Bloomsbury House
74–77 Great Russell Street
London WC1B 3DA

Typeset by Hamish Ironside
Printed in Great Britain by Martins the Printers
A CIP record for this book is available from the British Library

ISBN 978-0-571-31361-7

10 9 8 7 6 5

for Hannah

Acknowledgements

Thank you to the editors of following publications and websites where these poems were first published: *Best British Poetry 2014* (Salt, 2014), *BODY*, *Dear World and Everyone In It* (Bloodaxe, 2013), *Financial Times*, *Five Dials*, *Magma*, *Manhattan Review*, *The Moth*, *New Statesman*, *O Genesis Recordings*, *Oxford Poetry*, *Poetry London*, *Poetry Review*, *The Rialto*, *The Salt Book of Younger Poets* (Salt, 2011), *Smiths Knoll*, *Stop Sharpening Your Knives*, *Voice Recognition: 21 Poets for the 21st Century* (Bloodaxe, 2009), *The White Review*. I am grateful for the support of Arts Council England for a bursary in 2011, and to the Society of Authors for an Eric Gregory Award in 2007. I would like to thank Mum, Dad, Tom and my friends and Goldsmiths colleagues for their kindness and support. Special thanks are due to those who read drafts of these poems: Emily Berry, Sam Riviere, Hannah Bagshaw, Heather Phillipson, Katherine Kilalea, Sophie Robinson, Joe Dunthorne, Sophie Collins, Rachael Allen, Sam Buchan-Watts, Holly Pester, Wayne Holloway-Smith, Ben Pester and Luke Kennard; I am grateful to my tutors, Maura Dooley, Maurice Riordan, Lavinia Greenlaw, George Szirtes and Andrea Holland; my editor, Matthew Hollis, and Martha Sprackland at Faber.

Contents

HAPPINESS

Certain

Nothing before had seemed so potent
and self-contained –
surely the onion was beautiful.

Its hung cloud of acid worked
in his nose and throat
as the knife bisected

like a maker of names passing
between twins, calling one half *Perfect*
the other also *Perfect*.

Spring

       is here so now the plants and animals
are starting to have sex again. We've unblocked
the drain of its crud and bumf; the smell is waning.
We've washed the gravel, and piled the fox turds
in a far off corner. We are wearing slightly fewer clothes.
Our bodies, newly exposed, are strangers to themselves.
They chime against the air. A thought arrives of our life
together, yet to come. It configures like a beam of dust.
Look, this plant has made it through the winter you say,
as millions of photons whoosh through my hands.

Happiness

Yesterday it appeared to me in the form of two purple
elastic bands round a bunch of asparagus, which was
a very small happiness, a garden variety, nothing like
the hulking conversation cross-legged on a bed we had
ten years ago, or when I saw it as a thin space in a mouth
that was open slightly listening to a friend pinning them
with an almost-cruel accuracy; the sense of being *known*
making a space in their mouth that was happiness.
There was the happiness of my mother as we sat on
a London bus, her having travelled alone to visit her son,
and she seemed more present which might have been
the luggage I was carrying for her that weighed heavy
as her happiness, or was her happiness. It is rare you see
a happiness so nut-like as that which we permit my
father to pass around when he is talking sentimentally,
embarrassing us all. And of course, the goofy ten gallon
hats of happiness that children plant on us everytime
they impersonate knowledge. Or when I am standing on
a step breathing it in and out, staying death and the deadness
that comes after dying, sighing like a song about it. Or
privately with you, when we're watching television and
everyone else can be depressed as rotten logs for all we care,
because various and by degrees as it is, we know happiness
because it is not always usual, and does not wait to leave.

Sometimes your sadness is a yacht

huge, white and expensive, like an anvil
dropped from heaven: how will we get onboard,
up there, when it hurts our necks to look?

Other times it is a rock on the lawn, and matter
can never be destroyed. But today we hold it
to the edge of our bed, shutting our eyes

on another opened hour and listening
to our neighbours' voices having the voices
of their friends around for lunch.

William

at four days old

When the lock chucks familiar,
or a cat follows its name from a room,
when silence is strung, or rain
holds back the trees, I thought
I had the lever of these.
But weighing your fine melon head,
your innocent daring to be,
and mouth-first searching,
your tiny fist is allowed absolutely
and I am uncooked
– I can feel my socks being on –
utter, precious apple,
churchyards flatten in my heart,
I've never been brilliant so scared.

My Sister

Two summers ago when I was going nuts
I thought my sister's ghost lived in our garden.
My shoulders felt warm, and I confided.
Let me say she was real, then, as a tongue
you can bite. Let me say I knew she was
very good at hockey, and fun as a tent.
She painted roughly, but well, liked boys
with beards but not sex with boys with beards.
Her hands were the same size as mine.
Her voice seemed unaffected by gravity
and she would often discover herself
holding a table's attention. She told me
her ideal man was Picasso, and that her
biggest regret was not putting her name
firmly onto living, slipping beneath it
before she was born. And I regret it
in the garden with the dead fireworks,
my face going wet, everything crashed
on this wall, another summer coming on.

∞

After you, I will fall in love with someone
two or three hundred years older. Their heart
    will be a hole
in the church roof. For them, falling
will be like cutting a telephone wire and watching
    it swing
down into the street. If we have sex, I will take
    some annual leave
and position our pleasure like I'm setting up
a game of chess, and they will drop an apple on
    the floor
to clear all their weather away.
They will tire quickly of my nervousness,
my hurrying blood. It will not end well.
My lover will cut another wire, and perhaps you
    will find me
again, wandering the stump of a century, my eyes
    wide
as coconut halves, my heart the last hole your lace
    ties through.

Some Gods

God with eagle's head and five-pointed-star insignia on palms of hands; God connected to seven IV drips with fire coming out of mouth; God made of warts; God with horse's legs and head of ram reading names from a scroll pointing to a hole in the ground; God surrounded by representatives from the animal kingdom; God surrounded by representatives from the kingdom of global finance; God with cobbler's last and washing line with human faces pegged along; God with merciful expression holding knife and fork; God as a female infant; God with stomach as gumball machine; God as smiling coma patient between starchy cotton sheets surrounded by cards and flowers; God banging human skull-gavel to silence a courtroom of lesser gods; God being led into a courtroom and asked to confirm holy name; God in fool's attire inviting you to play a game of rummy; God as bronze medallist forcing smile on podium; God as golden ball of light forming in your chest; God as a feeling of intense and sudden cold; God as a feeling of sudden loneliness; God as a cup in your house that you haven't yet recognised as God but drink from nearly every day; God as a dead robin; God as the eye of a dead robin; God as your barely visible reflection in the eye of a dead robin.

Maths

To commemorate the grand bazaar
the king is given a prize goat (x)
that is one and a half metres high.
Given that a prize goat eats
ten square yards of grass a day,
how long should the leash (y)
be tied so the prize goat can roam free
and feed until the next bazaar?

To the man who can give an answer
in yards and show his working,
goes the talcum hand of the virgin princess
who is also one and a half metres high.

Men come. One brings a ball of string
and a cauliflower to show he is both wise
and humble, another swings a bag of seeds,
two brothers flex their matching red braces.

So the suitors measure, scribble, compare
their feats of mind, strength and faith.
Bunting feathers the eaves, a local man
juggles numbers through the streets
dressed in the fleece and horns of a buck.
The princess bites her lip, her hair plaited
with ribbons the colours of her country.
Meanwhile the goat goes hungry.

Toad

Toad, I have told you already,
this is not your house. Why do you insist
on staying there under the sink?
You cannot eat the soap like that,
it makes your insides sick.

I remember toad, the shed we used to sit in.
How in the fizzing light of a twenty-watt bulb
you were moved to unbutton love, to turn out
your pockets and inspect the lint and sand
in the oil palm of your toad hand.
You were friendly in the sawdust then,
your toad face wide as the brim of your hat.

You cannot eat the soap like that.
Toad, it makes my insides sick.

Love Poem

The streets look like they want to be frying eggs
on themselves. I'm thinking of you and going
itchy from it. I keep expecting to see a nosebleed
on the hot, yellow pavement. Every thought is
a horse fly. When you're not here I concentrate
on *getting somewhere safely*; and when I get to
somewhere safe I gnaw the day until you're home.

Second

for Toby Underwood

If I lived in a cave and you were my only visitor,
what would I tell you that the walls had told me?
That people are unfinished and are made between
each other, that worry is either a Mexican finger trap
or the revolving door to a hospital foyer, that love
is a feeling deferred, which is why it weighs negative
and sucks on you like a cruise ship disappearing?

I would probably warn you to never feel mystical:
nothing is mystical. I would tell you to let yourself
be sad, if being sad is what happens when a person,
awkward in the universe as a plum on a plate,
drops their day to the inaccessibility of other days,
and loosens their tie on the sofa to let some life out.

Poem of Fear for My Future Child

When I think about pushing your pram by the pond,
all the dogs off their leads, nothing between us and
the dark, weedy water, I drown you. I'm sorry.
I'm sorry I cannot save your soft head from the terrier
whose jaws lock, that I wasn't looking the second
you disappeared leaving me hot and turning round
for the man or any kind of words. And as you've grown
strong enough for kites and canoes or walks to shops
again, I'm sorry: I am such a dreadful future father;
I'm on the curb, crying, I'm a mess with your scarf.
All this fear, like a fizz building in a bad, grey egg,
is waiting for you. All this greenstick, nodular love,
so tense, perversely stored like a bubble in my lungs,
will be here, a huge trembling hand, when you arrive.

from Tenuous Rooms

If Thou Must Love Me

If you agree to LOVE me it has to be solely
on the basis of that thin ticket. Don't say
'I love him for the pockets at his mouth's edge' or
'because his voice is tomato soup and we share
the same taste in other people's shortcomings';
all of this stuff might change, or puncture.
Don't LOVE me because we are an endlessly
absorbent wad – we might not find we are very
sorry for each other. But LOVE me for a feeling
of risk that is real as the feeling we had standing
in the cathedral, looking up beneath the big chandelier.

The Good Morrow

I'm not sure I remember what we did
before we LOVED. Were we gherkins bobbing
in our harmless jars, with vinegar and seeds?
Or were we stuffed in a tube of sleep for years?
Probably; but that kind of life is carbohydrate.
If I enjoyed anything then it was feeling FULL.

The rover is making dust-ladder tracks on Mars.
The Victorian sewers have been overhauled, widened.
And here we both are, up-and-dressed.
But it's initimidating isn't it
when cack-handed LOVE is at his console,
nuking all life beyond this tenuous room.
I'm going to rely heavily on you, out there.

Holy Sonnets X

O drunk DEATH, go home. We like our dying lives.
Have a big glass of water and think about it:
I sleep in often. I waste my life like rain.

Canto XIII

Every single thought I'm having is about LOVE:
like the thought that I'd like to be LOVE's butler
or the one that says LOVE is just a spoon in a stew;
one is saying that desire itself is compelling,
while another puts snot up my wrists from crying.
All of them agree that they are sorry about my furniture
being madly rearranged to the floor-plan of my organs,
but overall I'm not sure which of them to trust:
which LOVE I want to explain or try to unpack,
to the point that I've forgotten what my job is.
If I want to get some cohesion, a treaty drawn up,
the process will have to be overseen (pathetically)
by my own self-pity in the form of a huge grey battleship.

I promise when I lift your egg

from the water with my special spoon,
carry it to a cup as if it were a bald man
whistling steam to a tune he had just made up;
when I take my green handled egg-knife
to whip off the top and inside it is more
than yellow, like a laugh about to happen,
or butter pushed into light; when you dunk
gorgeously in, softly exploding the yolk
like a new idea finding one coloured term
for its articulation; when the little promise
of the egg, contained inside from the moment
it was laid, is broken by your tongue, then,
like love, it is remade, I promise.

A man is dragging a dead dog

on a lead, down the street.
It makes a low-register hissing sound that is constant and
gives you a sense
of the weight of the dead dog. The lead is pulled tight to a
straight line.
It is attached to a collar which is the point of the freight
most forward,
the dog's head having been pinned beneath its body as it
moves along relatively
slowly against the pavement making that hissing sound.
The rearmost point
of the dead dog is what you might call, in this instance, its
'bottom leg'
because the pelvis has been rotated, the dog twisted on its
side, so one leg
is in full contact with the ground while the other is slightly
elevated and wobbles.

And since you already have a street in mind and perhaps
a breed of dog,
a colour of lead, or the kind of coat the man is wearing,
why not become
the man dragging a dead dog on a lead behind you? Why
not try
to understand this thing you are doing: how the dog came
to be dead
and you came to be dragging it, what this means to you
and where it is
that you are going?

An Avoidance

I could go around all evening dropping slices of lime
into other peoples' drinks, because it's easy to give
away fractions of happiness. But bad news ticks
in the kettle as it rests, and someone's dressed
as Death in the Halloween party photo, and
someone's dressed as Death in the birthday
party photo, class photo, front row, by the font
at the Christening . . . I should've called.
I should've called right away, welcomed your
sadness, taken it, pulled up a white plastic patio
chair, and said *I know you don't want to be here
either*. Instead I let a week pass. It was so easy.

Accidental Narratives

A crab on the phone box floor; the armless mannequin
on the chapel roof at dawn; the plastic toad in the office
biscuit tin; three cuts on your shin this morning to make
the letter A; the wedding cake abandoned in the car park
of the motorway services; the caraway seed in the turn-up
of your jeans, the waxwork head of Chaplin in the bowling
bag in the overhead locker of the night train to Munich;
a slug exposed by the spotlight of a hushed concert hall;
or the roaring magnificent intersection of these objects,
which probably never existed, but we can each picture,
drawn from our unique worlds at large, knocking like fish,
trying to agree; meanwhile, either somebody else somewhere
is reading this now, or no one else in the entire world is.

The Ashes

It's the first day of the second test of the Ashes series
and a voice on the radio is describing
the atmosphere here at Lord's without realising
that his voice describing the atmosphere
on the first day of the second test
is the atmosphere; it is his voice that will happen
to all of us listening in our cars
and our gardens, and I am in the kitchen.

Some recent news has changed my life a little
and as I run the sink, doubting for a second
that steam will appear, I consider my news
which widens into my narrative
like I'm stepping back from the edge of a lake,
and I picture, for some reason, a man
being wheeled into a room, eye-level with a bed
that he sees from the door and thinks
There is the bed I will die in. His deathbed
seems to know it too, but it has wheels and he hadn't
thought of that. They have him resting on the edge,
and twist him, lifting his legs around and a feeling
of resentment sinks through him because *they*
are putting *him* away, because *he* cannot put *himself*
away, and he does not want to be put away at all!
Death is happening *to* him and the players are out
on the field now, joining the umpires,
and in a few moments time the batsmen will be out
and the second test will be under way.
I've done the few dishes and cutlery and cups
and I'm wiping down the sink, then the side,

remembering what someone said last week:
You think about death a lot, don't you?
and I realise I've been doing it again.
But imagine you knew the objects to hand
were your last objects: like a TV remote:
the rubber buttons at the edge of your nail, or
you're rubbing its smooth back in your palm;
you're clicking open the back and rolling
the batteries, like two little buddies in there –
you are alive. You are alive and, I'm told, emitting light,
and here you are, and here you are, and here you
still are. Are. *That's why*, I think, *That's why*
I say out loud, as he's up to his mark now, in past
umpire Aleem Dar, because when I'm feeling unsteady
like this, the objects to hand become a cartoon chorus,
singing out to me 'Don't die today, don't leave
the house and fucking die' and the ball pitches
on a fullish length, and I'm choking my feeling back,
though I feel like a throat: sad and scared for a man
I've made-up to be myself, in a room on his final day
and there's no shot played as he lets this one go by.

The bomb

I sat on was room temp, smooth.
My balls rested on its neck; it was all neck,
apart from the fins that didn't look real,

and the nose which seemed to slide into nothing,
then further. And I could tell it had stringy,
warm guts; electric gristle stretched inside.

I felt proud of the bomb, scared and a little sexy.
I don't think I'm a bad person when I admit
I lent down and touched my face against it.

13 Say

When Neil Armstrong died you called me to your computer:
'Look! Of the 89 comments on the article, 13 say "he's on
the moon, now"! Why would he be *on the moon*? It's absurd!'
So I put my grandmother on the moon. I put Iain, who died,
on the moon with Hilary, who died. I put the great cats on
the moon, bouncing weightless and bemused; and I will put
all of us who are not dead but will be dead, on the moon,
which from here is a quiet place, out of reach and strange,
with a hard wind that rushes through: a rolling headstone
that requires a giant leap, and a sad and happy lie, to get to.

Sally and Rina

are talking on the balcony of the student union building. They are in the second year of their respective degrees (Rina, English Literature, Sally, English and American Literature) and their friendship has deepened over the past few months since Michael, Sally's housemate, has been seeing Rina on a more regular basis, and Sally and Rina have found themselves in more regular social contact. They have become close, but this closeness is still fresh with novelty. They are discussing a party that Rina left early with Michael the night before, and although Sally relays her anecdotes well, and selects only notable and entertaining details from the time following Rina's departure (of which there are many, the party being particularly well-attended and growing raucous largely towards the end) Rina cannot help but afford herself a moment of disconnect, or abstraction, in which she almost hears Sally's voice reduce slightly in volume, and in this moment Sally's face presents itself in a new way to Rina – not as her friend's face, but as a system of moving parts. It is at this point Rina feels an impulse drawing forwards in her mind, to punch Sally's face as hard as she can. The impulse hardens and shocks her. She worries that the shock of the thought has registered visibly on her own face, and is relieved to find that Sally, who is still ably telling her anecdote, is oblivious to the violent impulse, already rejected and repressed by her friend. Still, the shock of the impulse has distracted Rina. Why had this thought occurred? Rina clenches her fist a little, as if to regain control of her body, to make sure she can be certain she will not act upon the impulse. She likes

Sally, she reassures herself. This is simply an irrational glitch. Rina, feeling reassured, is now ready to fully engage in the anecdote, confident that for the duration of her inward detour she has appeared outwardly engaged and interested. She has said *Really?* and also furrowed her brow. This frown was initially an outward response to her worrying inner concerns, but Rina, registering some confusion on Sally's face (since that passage of anecdote did not especially warrant a frown), was able to pass it off as an expression of deep concentration, and so loosen her frown into a welcoming smile as if she were satisfied that a certain detail she had been unsure about had found a pleasing resolution. However, as Rina now tries to reengage with a renewed interest in Sally's story, in part motivated by a sense of guilt at her violent thought and subsequent betrayal of her friend in feigning interest, she finds she has lost track of the anecdote, or has at least missed a crucial part of its structure or rhetorical arc – the crux, she fears, on which the meaning of the story depends. As Sally increases her enthusiasm at what must surely be the denouement, Rina feels a sense of panic draw forwards in her, sensing that despite her best efforts to feign both surprise and comprehension she will betray the fact that she has not been listening, and Sally will realise her efforts have been expended without hope of reward, and will probably doubt herself, and her ability to tell an amusing anecdote, or worse, her friendship with Rina, who is only being further distracted by this sense of panic: that she will hurt her friend, that she will be thought of as disingenuous, that she is, indeed, relatively disingenuous compared to her friend, who in a matter of seconds will have good grounds on which to base that poor opinion of her. And this panic, Rina feels, is now registering outwardly on her face, and though it is possible Sally will read this as anticipation, Rina doubts she will do so for very long, as Sally's voice now seems entirely abstracted to Rina; only her bright expectant eyes are speaking and when they stop speaking what will Rina say? What can she possibly say?

Inventory of Friends

I run through the grass-topped lives of my friends:
I would like to have his body that is so slender
it looks sponsored by a company from Switzerland,
or that guy's gliding youth, his hopeful wardrobe:
I could use a transfusion of shyness to my voice.
I know ten people who are blessings: good people
for long car journeys, good people for talking to
on steps outside before we go in; or that twentieth
century seriousness that he has: I'd like a slice
of proper prowess. And I try to imagine having
her mind: funny, smart and odd as twenty
emperor penguins filing through the door
of a black limousine. But with a predictability
that would be cuteness if it weren't honest first,
my thoughts turn to you and what it might be
like to be so quietly impressive as a morning, or
a factory in the distance; what it might be like
not to have a clumsy great self always knocking,
what it might be like to be you, coming home
in four hour's time with no inkling of the way
my insides groan and click like a tired, old
galleon when you take off your coat like that.

The Anatomy of the Hammock

Once, in a hammock, life was a dogleg drive.
I had a worry in my chest like the bad layer
of an onion – I felt strung between two things:
I closed my eyes and I was moving.
I opened them and I was not.
We are nearing the conclusion of this anatomy.
We are strung between the point of ending and
the point of having started. Above me leaves layer up,
but do not hide the sky. Below me the ants move,
seemingly meaningful. Their little minds agree,
each like a high musical note. They arrive
from a hole I have no idea about, then disappear
down another such hole, I can only imagine.
I wonder about them. For some minutes.

The Spooks

I want to inject blood into the banana
then put it smartly in a bowl I want
someone to idly choose it peel it then taste
the strange rust a quarter way down
and spit it out see blood in the lemony mulch
(a sort of red spit with the tiny black seeds)
I want them to check their mouth for a source a cut
and by now the person they are with will be confused
(blood on the lip in the footwell
at the gum-edges) and say *are you ok?*
I want them to reply *there's blood* then without
even meaning to without a logical tracing
of thought look back to the banana and see
blood in the banana, feel the raw shock
of something possibly unthought of
I want them to get to the idea that
someone *put* the blood *in* the banana
an idea drinking heat from the skin but held
unable to understand to fit the reasons
I want this to happen.

My steak

               will be as thick
as the frown of the beast,
will be a cut kind of love.

When you cook it for me try
not to cook it, but weigh it
on a high heat until unstable.

Think of it as mud dying,
a pushed hand, or a question,
hung in itself, about blood.

I will unpack into my mouth
cud-grass, eye-roll, fathom
the taste of my own cow tongue.

Commend me to my steak
for I am a living beak
and all my teeth are hungry.

Caboose

The driver's hands sweat black juice and I never
see him eat. This caboose gets wider or shorter
depending on the way I'm lying. The gnats circle
above the latrine like they're going down a plughole.
All the moths are depressed. I have a dead moth
for an ex-wife, is the running joke between the driver
and the moths. This ladder can only lead to the sea.
Its miles pour out of me like sand from a shoe.
I ask the driver *how much further now?* and he
repeats it like the moth joke again. He refuses
to learn my name. Did I show you my magazine?
I've read it cover to cover, memorised key parts.
The faces are wearing out because there's nothing
else to read on here unless you like letters home.

from Solo for Mascha Voice

for Mascha Kaléko

Because Your Eyes

Because your eyes are always so topped up with rain
grief wears his day shoes and walks across the lawn.
Your forehead is a path I haven't the stomach to cross.
Let's sit and listen, instead, to all the missing songs.

Solo for Mascha Voice

As soon as you leave the room the rain turns
its volume up. Loneliness nudges me with its head.
I forgive you for ruining my life.

When we were young you bullied my architecture,
peered right in, and it wasn't fair, to do that.
These years since I have died from it.

Yes, I admit when you were mine I stood too close
at parties, but tell me how that's incorrect in love.
Tell me, and I promise I'll put these ornaments down.

Complicated Inner Mascha

I feel an antique-sounding wanderlust cranking up,
but when I stop writing it refers only to you.
Today I walked past the rock formation.
It did not loom without your smallness before it.
What will happen to us lurks behind mountains . . .
Our love might be hauled before an Emperor . . .
Our love might need a lawyer, might be a copyright
infringement, the way your voice kicks in my head.
Does happiness unwrap to what it promised?
I'm so tired of promising. O wake us up again,
won't you, when you've figured us out.

Letter of Health

My body is in debate: *This house believes*
that love is an enviable fever . . .
Last night my chest was an office on fire.
My pillow hurt. I couldn't save the documents.
Now it is day again. The room has furniture
and I have ins and outs, my liquids.

Is that the knife-grinder, grinding his knives
outside the window, or the sound
of my heart cooling down?
If I were in a novel you'd travel three days
by horse to see me. If you were in a novel
I'd die somewhere in these middle chapters.

Death says

the atoms of men have already spent infinity
as part of something else and all your human fudge
is the passing of a thread through the surface of a light.
If you are made of thinking, then being is a breath
    between the slats,
which is why I itch your collar when a fly taps the pane.
I am your address, and the hand that delivers you
    through.
I am the socket love must plug itself into.
I am the lie that runs along your ribs, the gap between
    the rock
and the wet place you will make there for yourself.
You will know my hand by the back of your own.
I am talking to you now in the voice you read with
    inwardly,
private as the name you say to the bottom of a tall
    felt hat.

Love Poem to Myself

Your basic appetites and pale feet renew
my faith in evolution; when you slide drunk
into a bath all the palm trees in Miami burn;
when I think about your nervous system,
its black market of strands, tearing electrics,
I feel outwardly stupid; *I love you*, I say, and
the room rings as if the air around my skin
were the rind of something citrus.

Theology

He tried to think about the zoo,
the bird he'd seen with an anvil head,
slinking lizards in the reptile house.
It had been a good day.

But he remembered the panther enclosure
where he had waited for thirty minutes,
staring up at a dark hut hidden in trees.
Suppose there was no panther.

Oversize

Compasses adjust to the clenching
of my cutlery. I am so big today I push
my finger to the earth's yolk and erupt it
like a boil. I read in my head and it rains
everywhere. My teeth make the moon
nervous. All things are near to me because
if I felt alone, or lost, the floor would fall
in space, and houses rush upwards.

If guns

were more popular in our culture
I'd be attracted to people who had guns the same way
I am attracted to people I suspect don't like me.

I would walk up to them shyly with my hands up
and ask for *a hold*. I'd say *Hollowpoint* or *Wadcutter*
as if they were the nicknames of our mutual friends.

It takes a certain person to shoot a certain person,
I would suppose, *With Great Power comes*
Great Guns. Can I look down the end?

I'd watch them slide out the clip and droop the gun
to me like a kneeling horse. I'd look in its hole,
blow my cheeks. *Thank you*, I'd say. *Thank you.*

Wilderbeast

In the wilderness the devil came to me:
big antique horns, a swinging red dick
and my father's angry voice.

He offered me grapes, a puckered teat
loose with wine and milk. I spat.
And he spat back, my mother's maiden name.

I pressed on, urged my feet. Satan changed tack;
swam me in sensation: my first time drunk,
the heat of a well spun lie, boyhood

glimpsed between a hairdresser's breasts,
the smell of shampoo and cigarette breath.
Then from a tuck in his arse he pulled rain

and a chip shop queue, the taste of shandy,
wet football boots dangled by the laces,
acorns and conkers tumbling from their spouts.

I gave a shout, a kind of grief escaping
and from astride his chin appeared
two slim girl's legs, akimbo his beard.

He opened his ripe mouth, folded his tongue back
and in, wriggling pleasure from himself,
stamping it out on the bare earth, braying.

I felt hunger folding in my gut.
The devil swung his hips, each jerk giving birth
to a pair of round, pert tits. *I am a good man!*

I railed and each flesh sack withered and slapped
on the ground, sizzled on the grit-heat of rock.
I heard waves, an ocean then. But it was Satan

shushing with a four-knuckled finger to his lips.
A breeze faltered and caught over, seabirds swung
in long arcs. The devil leaned in and touched me,

quietly, here and then here.
Softly he drew a perfect circle on the ground
bid me dream my mortal desire inside it.

I took out a photograph of you my love.
Showed him grace: fixed and flattened,
wrapped in a scarf and coat last week,

when the camera pinned you to the sea
and I watched it happen from behind the lens;
my breath holding you there a moment.

I showed the devil your photo and he wept.
Flies fell buzzing from his cheeks.
You tempted and turned him

and the sun strained to look
as the perfect circle became a pool of water,
hardened into a mirror,

the mirror I've been staring into since,
in our bathroom, in our flat,
with the wilderness of seconds between us.

∞

I had a dream about a car filling up with darkness.
You weren't there and neither was I. There was
no one inside. It was fine. And when I woke
I thought for the first time about the happiness
of the dead: how they'll never need fetching
a glass of water, how fear for them is a wrong
number calling, how we needn't lead them
through the cordon in red blankets,
how fixed and safe they are.

Weasel

So Weasel, it has come to this;
to your thighs like tall glasses of milk,
your biscuit hair,
eyes that are like any kind of deep water.
It has come to those coiled, snaking guts
we had when we were younger still –
those balled-up sock guts of an afternoon
stolen back from college.
It has come to the spastic, ticking urges
rising through skin at the simplest
repositioning of your weasel hips,
or the one in twenty-seven kisses
I might land about your mouth,
of the right temperature and diction.

Was I even hungry once for eating?
Were you ever not the end to all fasts?

She Loves You Like

She loves you like your hair smells proteinous; she loves you like pausing to move a snail somewhere safer in the rain; she loves you like milk is not like water; she loves you like the last seconds of a bottle being filled; she loves you like tennis played by amateurs; she loves you like tennis played by professionals; she loves you like a leg of lamb; she loves you like a hollowed pumpkin as the candle descends; she loves you like the delivery man's knock; she loves you like parents falling asleep wherever they are; she loves you like a plane refuelling; she loves you like the fuel inside the hose, which is clear, cold and flammable.

Your horse

has arrived and is bending himself into the room,
refolding his legs. I knuckle his nose,
which reminds me of the arm of a chair.

He is talking low and steady,
rolling back an eye towards his chestnut brain.
Man-words are climbing his long throat.

I show him to the bathroom
and he is embarrassed. Next he is looking
through your photo album.

There are more of me, than of him.
We are crunching on polo mints together
and remembering the way your body used to move.

You Are Definitely Coming, So Why Not Now?

after Akhmatova

Life is a frozen lamb: I'm waiting.
I have turned off the lights and been dramatic, opening doors.
Take any form you like.
Why not come thumping great chunks off us,
or cut our necks like bike locks,
or creep into our bodies like a smell in the fridge
or surprise our throats like a tune from the morning radio
that we'll notice we're singing the way you notice
a police car pulling up the drive?
I don't care how. The drains are gurgling,
the sky is a reservoir of wrong-headed questions. And eyes
that I love are losing their tournament.

Reading the Milk

Bronwyn may die in August,
an argument in parliament
will last all of July and late rain
rot the jackets of the beet.

No news therein of the website,
or the pilot scheme on floor five,
just the usual business of smokers
huddled round a lunch hour.

No clues as to how the garlic taste
is getting in the eggs, why Ed
isn't talking to me, and despite
my looking, no cure for diggers' knee.

But I glean this: our life will be
just fine: enough blood for the heart
to keep us edging, television light
for the days gone spare,

the table will stay put, coppers
stack down in the dish, your frown
keep pace, and everything you cook
contain a short black hair.

Thank You for Your Email

Two years ago I was walking up a mountain path
having been told of excellent views from the summit.
The day was clear and hot, the sky wide and cloudless.
There was only the sound of my breath, my boots treading,
and the faint clonking of cowbells back down the track.
What little wind there was on the climb soon dropped
as I reached the summit, as if it had been distracted
or called upon to cover events elsewhere. I drank eagerly,
catching my breath, and then took in the view, which was
as spectacular as I had been told. I could make out a tree,
a shrub, really (though it being so distant in the valley
below I couldn't say how high), silently on fire, the smoke
trailing a vertical black line before dissipating. I watched
the flames consume the whole shrub. No one came to stop it.
No one seemed to be around to see it, and I felt very alone.
From nowhere a great tearing came: a fighter-jet, low
and aggressive, ripped above me and, surprised, I dropped
on one knee and watched it zoom, bellowing overhead.
As it passed I saw a shred of something fall, a rag, spinning.
I shielded my eyes to see, bewildered and pinned watching
the object, the rag, gather its falling weight, its speed, until
it flumped down without a bounce, only ten footsteps
to my right. It was part of a white bird, a gull. No head,
just a wing and a hunk of body. No leg, or tail, just
the wing and the torso: purple and bloodied. A violent
puddle surrounded it, already mixing with the grit.
Ferrous blood wafted and I recoiled feeling suddenly
cold and very high up and the view swam madly: I saw
for a second the flaming tree as I staggered backwards
and became aware that I was sitting, I had fallen, but I felt
as if I was falling and falling still, my mind unable to

connect the events which were real and terrifying because
they were real, only now I think it was not, perhaps,
a mountain, it was not, perhaps, a shrub on fire, and not
a fighter-jet boring its noise through the sky, and I am
certain now, it was not me, or a wing or body of a broken
bird, but the fearful and forgotten things I've lied to myself
about, and to my friends, and to my family.